I0099000

Early Do I Seek Thee

31 Days of Seeking God in the Morning

Written by

Amber Bryant

Amber Bryant
Little Rock, AR

Copyright © 2016 Amber Bryant. All rights reserved. No portion of this book may be reproduced mechanically, electronically, or by any other means, including photocopying, without written permission of the publisher. It is illegal to copy this book, post it to a website, or distribute it by any other means without permission.

Editing and Layout: Robin Devonish, The Self-Publishing Maven
Formatting: Suzette Vaughn
Book Cover: Jose Julian Ramirez and Okomota, The Design Lab

Limits of Liability
The author and publisher shall not be liable for your misuse of this material. This book is strictly for informational and educational purposes.

Disclaimer
The purpose of this book is to educate and entertain. The author and/or publisher do not guarantee that anyone following these techniques, suggestions, tips, ideas, or strategies will become successful. The author and/or publisher shall have neither liability nor responsibility to anyone with respect to any loss of damage caused, or alleged to be caused, directly or indirectly by the information contained in this book.

ISBN 13: 978-0-692-78947-6
ISBN 10: 0-692-78947-2
Printed in the United States of America

Let the morning bring me word of your unfailing love, for I have put my trust in you. Show me the way I should go, for to you I entrust my life.

– Psalms 143:8

Dedication

I dedicate this book to my mother, Phyllis Johnson. I love you mommy! Thank you for being patient with me and for your daily encouragement during this entire process!

Acknowledgments

First and foremost, I would like to acknowledge God. Thank you Lord for giving me the vision, the discipline, and the revelations to write this book. This script is for your glory and for the men and women that desire to seek you and seek you early.

To my parents, Phyllis Johnson, Vincent Johnson Sr., and Darrell Bryant, thank you for your unconditional love and support. I love you all dearly! I pray I continue to make you proud.

To my beloved grandmother, Janice James, thank you for your unyielding support and believing in my dream. Since I was a child, you have instilled into me wisdom, grace, and love. You are the wisest and strongest person I know. I love you granny!

To my Paw Paw, Cleaster Bryant, thank you for being one of the greatest men I have ever known!

To the best God-daddy in the world, Dwayne Yarbrough, thank you for always believing in me and loving me. Your love warms my heart! I love you so much!

To my bestie, Kelia Harris, thank you for your daily encouragement, love, and support. In my darkest hour, it was your words spoken by the Holy Spirit that motivated me to complete this book. I love you!

To my big sissy, Rory Hill, you are the best friend in the entire world! Your friendship is truly a gift from God! Thank you for being my rock! Your daily words of wisdom and encouragement have helped me more than you will ever know! I love you!

To my favorite uncle and aunt, Napoleon and Caron Williams, your love and spiritual strength never cease to amaze me. Thank you for your continuous support, encouragement, and guidance. I love you both!

To my siblings, Vincent Johnson Jr., Adrian Bryant, and Jenipher Bryant, I love you three very dearly.

To my cousin, Alana Hervey, thank you for your support in my dream! Your little sour is being very sweet! I love you!

To all my family and friends who have supported me during this journey, I love you all very much! Every prayer, word of encouragement, and financial donation has aided in the birth of this book.

Last and not least, to my awesome Self-Publishing Consultant, Robin Devonish. Thank you for being a wonderful guide and mentor to me during the writing and post-production of this book. Your Periscope videos were the motivation I needed to finish this script! Robin, thank you, and I love you.

Table of Contents

Introduction

"God is in the midst of her; she will not be moved; God will help her when morning dawns." –Psalms 46:5

With tears streaming down my eyes, I laid in the middle of the living room floor and cried out to God. In a muffling voice, I uttered, "Lord, Help me." The pain of a broken heart crippled me and left me paralyzed. I had no one to turn to and nowhere to go. I was all alone. My family and friends told me to get over it and move on, but it wasn't that easy for me. I tried. I really tried but I just couldn't. Sadness and despair became my companions. Misery became my company.

Proverbs 18:14 says, "A man's spirit will endure sickness, but a crushed spirit who can bear?" I had endured many sicknesses in my day, but the betrayal and agony of a broken heart felt unbearable. I tried everything I could to heal it, but nothing seemed to work until I cried out to God early one morning.

It was in the pitch blackness and right before the morning sun dawned, that my entire life changed. Awaken by the intense pain of heartache, I got up and finally said enough was enough. I was tired of crying myself to sleep every night. I was tired of living with misery, sadness, and despair. That morning I made up in my mind to seek the one and the only person that could help me. And His name is God! All my life I was taught weeping may endure for a night, but joy comes in the morning (Psalms 30:5). My night had lasted for far too long. It was time for some joy.

Before that particular morning, I can honestly say I knew of God, but I didn't know Him. I didn't have a personal relationship with Him. Like most Christians, I attended church faithfully every Sunday, but the rest of the week I didn't spend any time with Him. I didn't read my Bible nor did I praise or worship Him. However, I considered myself a Christian. Sound familiar?

Going to church regularly doesn't make you a Christian. The heart of Christianity is to seek and become more like Christ every day. God desires a personal relationship with all of us. He wants us to seek Him all the time; when times are good and when times are bad. James 4:8 says, "Draw near to God, and he will draw near to you." Day after day God searches the whole earth looking for people to love Him. People who desire Him above everything and everyone else in their lives. God is looking for you, but the question is will He find you?

Every day that we get to open our eyes and bask in the sunrise of a new day is a gift. A gift that our Heavenly Father bestows upon us because He still has a purpose for us to fulfill on this earth. The gift of a new day should never be taken for granted. The best way to show God we appreciate the daily gift of life is to seek Him wholeheartedly and make Him the most important priority in our lives.

For two years I took the gift of life for granted. I lived in constant pain and heartache every day. All I did was go to work, school, and church. I had the "Woe Is Me" syndrome but one morning I had an encounter with God that changed my life forever. For the first time in my life, I sought God, and He answered me. The Bible tells us that if we seek God with all our heart and soul, we will find Him (Deuteronomy 4:29).

That morning I found God in the midst of my despair. As I laid on the living room floor crying my heart out, God laid there with me. Psalm 34:18 says, "The LORD is close to the brokenhearted; he rescues those whose spirits are crushed." After that morning, I sought God more and more every day. Slowly but surely, He healed my broken heart. Not only did He heal my broken heart but He revealed Himself to me in a mighty and powerful way that I had never experienced before. When we spend time in God's presence daily, He reveals different layers of Himself to us. It's in the seeking of Him that we get to know Him.

After God restored my broken my heart, I developed a personal relationship with Him and made Him the first priority in my life. No one and nothing comes before God in my life. To show Him this, I began a daily journey of seeking Him in the morning. Every morning when I wake up, I start my day off with meditation, praise, worship, prayer, and Bible study.

To inspire others to take this journey with me, God gave me the vision to write this book. If you desire a closer relationship with God, this devotional is for you. Seeing this book is not an accident. God has been whispering softly in your ear, "Seek my face" (Psalms 27:8). Will you seek Him?

Over the next 31 days, prepare your mind, soul, body, and spirit to take a journey with God. Make a commitment to put God first and give Him the first few minutes of your morning. Seek Him early and seek with Him an expectation to receive a fresh Word of inspiration. It's time. Let the journey begin!

Day 1: Seek Ye First

"Seek the Kingdom of God above all else, and live righteously, and he will give you everything you need."
–Matthew 6:33

There is no one and nothing in this life you need more than God. As men and women of God, it is important that we remember God should be the first priority in our lives. Understand, our God, is a jealous God. Therefore, we should not place anyone or anything before Him. In fact, our first and greatest commandment is to love the Lord with all our heart, soul, and strength (Deuteronomy 6:5).

God's greatest desire is that we seek and love Him above all else. God wants sovereignty over every area in our lives. Make God first place in your life and He will provide you with everything you need. The Bible tells us in Psalms 34:10, "But those who seek the LORD lack no good thing."

Our Lord and Savior Jesus Christ taught us the key to a meaningful life on this earth is to seek God first and live righteously (Matthew 6:33). The greatest way to show God He reigns first in your life is to give Him the first few minutes of your day. Start your day off with worship, praise, and prayer. Get in His

presence and meditate on His Word. Seek His face and
He will show Himself unto you.

*I seek the Kingdom of God above everything and
everyone in my life.*

Day 2: At the Break of Dawn

"In the morning, long before sunrise, Jesus went to a place where he could be alone to pray." –Mark 1:35

Every day at the break of dawn Jesus would get up and go off into a deserted area and pray. During the quiet stillness of the morning when it was just Him and His Father, Jesus poured out His heart in prayer. The Bible tells us that those who seek Him early shall find Him (Proverbs 8:17). Before you start your daily morning routine, seek God in prayer.

So often we get busy in the hustle and bustle of our daily activities that we neglect to pray. When we don't start off our day with prayer, we leave the door wide open for the enemy to prey on us.

Prayer in the morning sets the tone for our entire day. In prayer, God gives us the strength, wisdom, provision, and protection we need to make it throughout the day. It is vital to our daily Christian walk that we give God the first portion when we open our eyes. Like Jesus, seek Him early!

Early will I seek Thee, before the morning dawns.

Day 3: Today Is The Day

"A new day will dawn on us from above because our God is loving and merciful." –Luke 1:78

Someone once asked me what my favorite day of the week was. To the person's astonishment, I answered, "Today!" While most people would have answered Friday, Saturday or Sunday, my favorite day of the week is any day I am alive! Every day that the Lord allows me to open my eyes and bask in the glory of a new morning is a gift. Some of us take this gift for granted.

The fact that you're reading this devotional right now is a testament to God's unconditional love, grace, and mercy towards you. Someone didn't make it last night, but you did. Alone, that is a reason to praise God! Even if you are going through a rough time right now, take comfort in this promise, "Here on earth you will have many trials and sorrows. But take heart, because I have overcome the world" (John 16:33).

In spite of what you may be going through, you can still delight in this day! In the words of King David, "This is the day that the Lord has made; let us rejoice and be glad in it" (Psalms 118:24). Today is the day! A new day that our Heavenly Father has bestowed His gracious love and kindness upon us! Rejoice, I say, and be glad in it!

Today is a new day, and I will rejoice and be glad in it.

Day 4: New Mercies

"It is of the LORD'S mercies that we are not consumed, because his compassions fail not. They are new every morning: great is thy faithfulness."
–Lamentations 3:22-23

Everyone deserves a second chance. A do-over. A fresh start. We all make mistakes and fall short of the glory of God. The Bible tells us in Ecclesiastes 7:20, "Not a single person on earth is always good and never sins." In spite of our daily shortcomings, God gives us brand new mercies every morning. Because of His unfailing love, compassion, grace and mercy, every day we have the opportunity to start over.

Let go of yesterday's burdens. Release the pain, guilt, shame, anger, sadness, and heartache. Give them to the Lord, and He will take care of you (Psalms 55:22). Though you may have wept all night long, this morning God wants to impart into you His joy, His peace, and His love. Receive His new mercies, grace, and blessings. Every morning thank Him for His kindness and every evening rejoice in His faithfulness (Psalms 92:2).

If you ever need something to be thankful for, be thankful that God's mercy endures forever! Micah 7:18 says, "Who is a God like you, who pardons sin and forgives the transgression of the remnant of his inheritance? You do not stay angry forever but delight to show mercy."

Lord thank you for your brand new mercies.

Day 5: Day and Night

"Rather, he delights in the teachings of the LORD and reflects on his teachings day and night." –Psalms 1:2

How did Jesus overcome Satan's temptations in the wilderness? He overcame him by the Word of God! When Satan tried to tempt Jesus to turn stones into bread, He answered him, "It is written, "Man shall not live by bread alone, but by every word that comes from the mouth of God" (Matthew 4:4). While food sustains our physical body, God's Word sustains our spirit man. We need the Word of God like we need air.

Reading God's Word should be a part of our daily spiritual regimen. Joshua 1: 8 says, "Study this Book of Instruction continually. Meditate on it day and night, so you will be sure to obey everything written in it. Only then will you prosper and succeed in all you do." The more we have the Word of God stored up in our hearts, the more we will believe, do, and live by what it says. In Psalms 119:11 King David said, "I have hidden your word in my heart, that I might not sin against you."

Fill yourself up with God's Word every day and watch your life dramatically improve. As you meditate on God's Word, you will begin to recognize God's will for your life. If you have been wavering in your faith, that's a sign you need to increase your Word intake. I recommend three dosages of reading the Bible a day! Your faith will grow stronger, and your fears will decrease. Read a few passages of scripture in the morning, on your lunch break, and at night before you go to bed. Meditate on the Word of God day and night!

I will meditate on the Word of God day and night.

Day 6: Command Your Morning

"Have you commanded the morning since your days began, and caused the dawn to know its place that it might take hold of the skirts of the earth, and the wicked be shaken out of it?"
–Job 38: 12-13

Do you know as a child of God you have the authority to command your morning by speaking God's Word? Our lives are created by the words we speak. When God wants something to be birthed or manifested, He speaks it into existence. Psalms 33:9 says, "For when he spoke, the world began! It appeared at his command." As His children, we have the same power to speak those things that are not as though they were (Romans 4:17).

Today can turn out to be one of the best days of your life, or it could turn out to be one of the worst. What you speak into the universe will determine that. Death and life are in the power of your tongue, and you will eat its fruits (Proverbs 18:21). So why eat the fruits of death when you can speak life? Every day when you wake up, you have the power to choose life by speaking God's promises over yourself. Whatever you decree and declare by faith shall be established unto you (Job 22:28).

Here are some examples of faith declarations you can use:

- I am healed, I am blessed, and I have the victory in Jesus Christ. (1 Corinthians 15:57)
- I can do all things through Christ who strengthens me. (Philippians 4:13)
- I walk by faith and not by sight. (2 Corinthians 5:7)
- I will overcome all attacks of the enemy by the Blood of the Lamb and the word of my testimony. (Revelations 12:11)
- All things will work together for my good today because I love the Lord, and I am called according to His purpose. (Romans 8:28)
- The Lord gives me strength and blesses me with peace. (Psalms 29:11)
- The Lord is my helper, and I shall not fear. (Psalms 118:6)
- God will supply all my needs according to His riches in glory by Christ Jesus. (Philippians 4:19)

You don't have to accept anything in your life that does not line up with the Word of God. Don't allow things to happened to you, make things happened through your authority as a child of God. Let the redeemed of the Lord say so (Psalms 107:2)!

I command my morning to be blessed and prosperous.

Day 7: Sufficient is the Day

"Therefore do not worry about tomorrow, for tomorrow will worry about itself. Each day has enough trouble of its own." –Matthew 6:34 NIV

Don't miss today's sunshine by worrying about tomorrow's rain. Have you ever checked the weather forecast and saw that it was going to rain the next day, and you started worrying? Maybe your child had an athletic activity that was supposed to be outside, and you worried about cancellation due to the rain. Instead of focusing on that day's sunshine, you consumed your mind with worry and stress over a day that has not happened yet.

Jesus instructs us not to worry about tomorrow because each day will have its own set of troubles (Matthew 6:34). Each day will have its own successes, failures, victories, defeats, challenges, and problems. Therefore, it is essential we focus our thoughts, energy, and time on today. Sufficient is the day.

You cannot foresee tomorrow nor can you control how it will turn out. James 4:14 says, "How do you know what is going to happen tomorrow? For the length of your lives is as uncertain as the morning fog—now you see it; soon it is gone." At any given moment God could call you home to be with Him. Do you want your last thoughts to be filled with worry about the future or happiness about today?

Stop worrying about what's going to happened tomorrow, next week or a month from now. Worrying about tomorrow will only rob you of today's joy, energy, strength, and peace. Focus on today.

I will live in the moment and trust God to take care of me.

Day 8: Daily Bread

"Give us this day our daily bread." –Matthew 6:11

Anyone who claims to be a Christian or is familiar with Christianity has heard of the Lord's Prayer. It is a simple prayer Jesus taught His disciples in Luke 11: 2-4:

> And the Word says, "And Jesus said unto them, When ye pray, say, Our Father, which art in heaven, Hallowed be Thy name. Thy kingdom come. Thy will be done on earth, as it is in heaven. Give us this day our daily bread. And forgive us our debts, as we forgive our debtors. And lead us not into temptation, but deliver us from evil: For thine is the kingdom, and the power, and the glory, forever."

Though the prayer seems to be simple, every line in that prayer is significant to our daily Christian walk. The Lord's Prayer is a model prayer that teaches us how to address our Heavenly Father effectively and ask Him for our daily needs.

In the third line of the prayer, we ask God to give us our daily bread. What exactly is our daily bread? In John 6, Jesus talks about the importance of seeking the "true bread of life" and tells a crowd of people, "I am the bread of life. Whoever comes to me will never go hungry, and whoever believes in me will never be thirsty" (v.35a). Jesus is our daily bread. In Him, we have everything we need to survive in this life.

Today and every day ask the Lord to give you your daily bread. As long as you seek the "true bread of life" you will be provided with everything you need. Pray 'The Lord's Prayer' daily! Let it be your guide and model on how to properly petition the Lord in prayer.

Lord give me this day, my daily bread.

Day 9: Sacrifice of a Praise

"Through Jesus, therefore, let us continually offer to God a sacrifice of praise--the fruit of lips that openly profess his name." –Hebrews 13:15

Has there ever been a time in your life when you didn't feel like praising God? Be honest, you don't praise God every day. You know you should, but some days instead of giving Him the praise He deserves you allow your problems to make you wallow up in self-pity. It can be difficult to praise God when you are in emotional turmoil.

Never allow your emotions to hinder your praise to God. No matter what's going on in our lives, God is always worthy of our praise. King David taught us to bless the Lord at all times and praise His name continuously. (Psalms 34:1).

In Psalms 54:6 King David said, "I will sacrifice a voluntary offering to you; I will praise your name, O Lord, for it is good." To give God a sacrifice of praise means to praise Him regardless of how you feel. Our feelings are temporary and fleeting, but God is constant and deserves our praises.

Praise God when you get up in the morning, throughout the day, and before you go to bed. Praise Him for what He has done, is doing, and will do in your life. Give God the honor, glory, and praise due to His name because He inhabits our praises (Psalms 22:3).

I will praise the Lord at all times.

Day 10: True Worshiper

"Come, let us bow down in worship, let us kneel before the LORD our Maker." – Psalms 95:6

In this hour God is looking for true worshippers, worshippers who worship Him in spirit and in truth (John 4:24). Are you that type? God is looking for people with a heart for Him. Hearts that yearn to seek Him and worship Him day and night. Hearts that worship Him not only for what He has done but simply for who He is.

So who is God? The Word tells us, "His understanding is beyond comprehension" (Psalms 147:5). God told Moses to tell the Israelites "I AM WHO I AM" sent you (Exodus 3:14). The Bible refers to God by many names, and each of His names describe one of His attributes of power. Some of His names include:

Jehovah Jireh (The Lord Will Provide)
Jehovah Shalom (The Lord Is Peace)
Jehovah Sabaoth (The Lord of Hosts)
Jehovah Nissi (The Lord My Banner)
Jehovah-Raah (The Lord My Shepherd)
Jehovah Rapha (The Lord That Heals)

When we worship God for who He is, He reveals Himself to us. If you want a closer relationship with

God, worship Him! Your worship will usher in His presence, and there is nothing greater on this earth than the presence of God. Worship Him in spirit and in truth.

I worship God in spirit and in truth.

Day 11: Confession

"I made my sins known to you, and I did not cover up my guilt. I decided to confess them to you, O Lord. Then you forgave all my sins." –Psalms 32:5

No one on this earth is perfect. We all have sinned and fallen short of the glory of God (Romans 3:23). No matter how righteous and holy we try to live we will be tempted to sin. Our spirit is willing to obey God, but our flesh is weak (Mark 14:38) and wants to give into its evil desires and lusts.

Apostle Paul describes our battle with sin in Romans 8:21-25:

"I have discovered this principle of life—that when I want to do what is right, I inevitably do what is wrong. I love God's law with all my heart. But there is another power within me that is at war with my mind. This power makes me a slave to the sin that is still within me. Oh, what a miserable person I am! Who will free me from this life that is dominated by sin and death? Thank God! The answer is in Jesus Christ our Lord. So you see how it is: In my mind, I want to obey God's law, but because of my sinful nature I am a slave to sin."

God knows, in spite our best efforts, sometimes we will lose our battle with sin. That is why Jesus died for us and was "raised to life to make us right with God" (Romans 4:25). When we sin, we must immediately ask God for forgiveness and repent.

In 1 John 1:9 Jesus says, "If we confess our sins, he is faithful and just and will forgive us our sins and purify us from all unrighteousness." Confession of our sins brings forgiveness, grace, and mercy but unconfessed and unrepented sin brings punishment and separates us from God (Isaiah 59:2).

It is vital to your daily Christian walk that you confess your sins daily. Don't let unconfessed sins be the reason why your prayers aren't being answered. Take this scripture in Proverbs 28:13 to heart, "Whoever conceals their sins does not prosper, but the one who confesses and renounces them finds mercy."

I confess my sins to you Oh, Lord and ask for your forgiveness.

Day 12: Forgiving Heart

"But when you are praying, first forgive anyone you are holding a grudge against, so that your Father in heaven will forgive your sins, too." –Mark 11:25

One day while walking with Jesus Peter asked Him how many times in a day did he have to forgive someone who sinned against him. Before Jesus answered him, Peter asked, "Up to seven times" (Matthew 18:21)? To Peter's amazement Jesus replied, "not seven times, but seventy-seven times" (Matthew 18:22)! It doesn't matter if a person hurts you over and over again, you have to forgive them.

When we pray the Lord's prayer, we recite "and forgive us our sins, as we have forgiven those who sin against us" (Matthew 6:12). To receive forgiveness from God, we must be willing to give it. God forgives us because He loves us. Think about all the times we have sinned against God and others. Each time we ask God for forgiveness and repent He forgives us. We must extend that same forgiveness to those who have sinned against us.

After being humiliated, beaten, tormented, and nailed to the Cross, Jesus uttered the most powerful forgiveness prayer ever spoken, "Father, forgive them; for they know not what they do" (Luke 23:34). If Jesus can forgive the Jews (His own people) for crucifying Him, we can forgive those who hurt us. After all, it was because of His crucifixion we have the redemption of our sins.

Every day we have to practice the act of forgiving. The scripture tells us in Ephesians 4:32, "Be kind to one another, tenderhearted, forgiving one another, as God in Christ forgave you." As the great Christian author, C.S. Lewis said it best, "To be a Christian means to forgive the inexcusable because God has forgiven the inexcusable in you."

I forgive anyone that has offended me and I extend grace, mercy, and love.

Day 13: As A Man Thinks

"Do not conform to the pattern of this world, but be transformed by the renewing of your mind. Then you will be able to test and approve what God's will is--his good, pleasing and perfect will." –Romans 12:2

You cannot live a positive life with a negative mind nor can you live a godly life with a worldly mindset. As Christians, we must renew our minds in the Word of God daily (Ephesians 4:23). What we think about we become and if we want to become more like Christ we have to think like Him. The Word tells us, "As a man thinks, so is he." (Proverbs 23:7)

Renewing our minds require that we purposely train our thoughts on Christ. Philippians 4:8 says, "Fix your thoughts on what is true, and honorable, and right, and pure, and lovely, and admirable. Think about things that are excellent and worthy of praise." Our thoughts can easily drift off into in the cares of this world and on ungodly desires and pleasures.

Renewing our minds takes discipline and focus. When ungodly and negative thoughts creep in your mind, immediately cast them out and bring them into the obedience of Christ (2 Corinthians 10:5). Control your thoughts or your thoughts will control you. Always remember what you think you become.

I will renew my mind in the Word of God daily.

Day 14: Secret Place

"He that dwelleth in the secret place of the most High
shall abide under the shadow of the Almighty."
–Psalms 91:1

There is a place that God wants you to go; a scared, quiet place where only you and He can dwell. In that place, you will pray to Him and He will answer you. In that place, He will speak to you, and you will listen. In that place, He will fill you up with love, joy, peace, and strength. Don't you desire to go to that place; the secret place?

It is recorded several times throughout the New Testament that Jesus would often slip off into the wilderness and pray by Himself for hours. Before Jesus would go out and preach the Gospel or perform any miracles, He would go to His secret place and fellowship with His Father. In His secret place, He received the power He needed to complete His daily assignments.

While we can pray anywhere and at any time, the secret place requires us to go into a deeper level of intimacy with God. A level where only God can fulfill and meet our needs, wants, and desires. Some people call this place the prayer closet. Others call it the War Room. It doesn't matter what you call it. It just matters that you go. The Father is waiting for you. He is expecting you. Will you go to the secret place?

I will dwell in the secret place of the Most High.

Day 15: Be Still

"Stand in silence in the presence of the Sovereign Lord." –Zephaniah 1:7

To truly hear from God, you have to unplug from the world. You have to put your phone down, cut off your TV, and get in a quiet place and be still. The Word tells us in Ecclesiastes 3:7, there is a "time to keep silence, and a time to speak." Sometimes you speak in the presence of the Lord and other times you keep silent and be still. Sitting still before the Lord takes discipline, focus, and obedience. Being still doesn't come naturally to us. It is something we have to train our minds to do.

In Psalms 46:10 God tells us to, "Be still, and know that I am God." To know God, you have to get in His presence. When you get in His presence, don't speak just listen. God knows what you need. He knows how you feel. He knows everything. Just sit silently before Him and let Him speak to your spirit.

God speaks to us in a still, small voice. He doesn't yell nor does He scream. If you are not intently listening to hear from Him, you will miss His voice. Don't miss the voice of God. Learn the art of being still and quiet so God can give you fresh revelations, wisdom, and knowledge. Get in His presence today and be still!

I sit in silence in the presence of the Lord.

Day 16: He Will Answer

"But I, O LORD, cry to you; in the morning my prayer
comes before you." –Psalms 88:13

What is the first thing you do when you wake up in the morning? Naturally, most people use the bathroom, then, they proceed with the same mundane, routine. They brush their teeth, get their kids ready for school, eat breakfast and then head off to work. Seeking God and praying is usually the last thing on their mind. But what about you?

King David woke up every morning with anticipation to pray to God. Psalms 5:3 says, "In the morning, O Lord, hear my voice. In the morning I lay my needs in front of you, and I wait." Every morning King David laid his petitions before God in prayer and then patiently waited for Him to reply back to him.

Many can miss the mark in prayer by not waiting on God to speak back. Prayer in its simplest definition is a conversation with God. When we pray, we should expect for God to answer us back. Though we might not always like His answers, He will answer.

Every morning before you start your daily routine make it your number one priority to spend time with God in prayer. God is ready to hear from you and grant your requests. Cry out to Him and tell Him your needs and wants, and then patiently wait for Him to answer you back. Like I said before, He will!

The Lord will answer my prayer.

Day 17: Are You Missing The Mark?

"For all who are led by the Spirit of God are sons of God." –Romans 8:14

How do you know if you are truly a child of God? What distinguishes you from an unbeliever? Just because you identify yourself as a Christian does not make you one. What makes you a son or daughter of the Most High God? The answer lies in 2 Corinthians 1:22, "He has put his brand upon us—his mark of ownership—and given us his Holy Spirit in our hearts as a guarantee that we belong to him and as the first installment of all that he is going to give us."

The mark of Christianity is being filled with the Holy Spirit. The Holy Spirit is the Spirit of God that lives inside of us, and His job is to lead and guide our lives. To live a godly life, you must be filled with the Holy Spirit. We need the Holy Spirit's assistance to help us make the right decisions according to God's Word.

Before Jesus ascended to heaven, He said, "When the Spirit of Truth comes, he will guide you into the full truth. He won't speak on his own. He will speak what he hears and will tell you about things to come" (John 16:13). He speaks on God's behalf to us and on our behalf to God.

Every day we battle against our flesh. In Galatians 5:17 Apostle Paul said, "The sinful nature wants to do evil, which is just the opposite of what the Spirit wants. And the Spirit gives us desires that are the opposite of what the sinful nature desires. These two forces are constantly fighting each other, so you are not free to carry out your good intentions." The only way to combat our flesh is to walk in the Spirit.

The Holy Spirit enables us to live holy and righteous. Our desire to do good doesn't come from us, but from the Spirit of God that lives inside of us. The true seal of being a Christian is being filled and led by the Holy Spirit. Are you letting the Holy Spirit lead and guide your life? Jesus left the Holy Spirit as our comforter, teacher, and guide (John 14:26). Make sure you are marked!

I am led by the Holy Spirit.

Day 18: The Need to Intercede

"I urge you, first of all, to pray for all people. Ask God
to help them; intercede on their behalf, and give
thanks for them." –1 Timothy 2:1

Your greatest service as a Christian is to pray for
others. As Christians, we are called to bear the burdens
of others in prayer (Galatians 6:2). It is through our
prayers that God can intervene in the lives of others.
Understand, there will be no intervention from God
without our intercession. Our prayers enable God to
perform His will on earth as it is in heaven (Matthew
6:10).

There are so many people around you in
desperate need of your prayers. How often do we
complain about our families and friends' problems
without praying for them? Instead of helping and
praying for them, we criticize and judge them. Maybe
the reason why they are still in that bad marriage,
financial distress, low-paying job, or living in
depression is because you haven't interceded to God
on their behalf. God will intervene when you intercede.

How many people do you know that need to
confess Jesus as Lord? Have you prayed for their
salvation? Never take for granted the responsibility
and power of intercession. Every day Jesus sits at the
right hand of the Father and intercedes on our behalf

(Romans 8:34). If Jesus can pray for others every day, so can we. The "earnest prayer of a righteous person has great power and produces wonderful results" (James 5:16). Imagine how many lives could be changed by your prayers.

I will pray for others.

Day 19: Order My Steps

"Let me hear of your unfailing love each morning, for I am trusting you. Show me where to walk, for I give myself to you." –Psalms 143:8

When we wake up in the morning, we have no idea how our day is going to turn out, but God does. We can make all the plans we want, but at the end of the day, the Lord's plans will always prevail over our own (Proverbs 19:21). Therefore, why not just ask Him for His plans! The Word tells us that steps of a good man are ordered by the Lord (Psalms 37:23).

When we fully submit ourselves to God He will direct and our guide our lives. In Psalms 32:8 He tells us, "I will guide you along the best pathway for your life. I will advise you and watch over you." God is our personal GPS. While navigating through life, we need His directions. Without Him leading our lives, we are bound to make wrongs turns. How many wrong turns have you made in your life that led you on a dead end street? I am sure more than you would like to count!

Stop trying to figure everything out and trust God to order your steps. Proverbs 20:24 says, "Since the Lord is directing our steps, why try to understand everything that happens along the way?" Life will always throw curve balls at you. You might stumble.

You might even fall, but when the Lord is ordering your steps you will always get back up!

Lord order my steps in your Word.

Day 20: Humble Spirit

"Do nothing out of selfish ambition or vain conceit.
Rather, in humility value others above yourselves."
–Philippians 2:3

Jesus came to this earth and took up the nature of a servant by putting others' needs before His own. "For even the Son of Man came not to be served but to serve others and to give his life as a ransom for many" (Matthew 20:28). Throughout His time on earth, Jesus embodied the greatest Christian characteristic, which is, humility! When we walk in the spirit of humility we show that we are true children of God.

The root of humility is selflessness. A humble spirit is intent on doing the will of God and putting others' needs before its own. When we walk in the spirit of humility we love our neighbors as we love ourselves. We strive daily to help, encourage, uplift, and inspire our fellow brothers and sisters in Christ in any we can.

Besides selflessness, a humble spirit also exemplifies the nine virtues of the Holy Spirit. The Bible calls these virtues the fruit of the spirit and they are love, joy, peace, patience, kindness, goodness, faithfulness, gentleness, and self-control (Galatians 5:22-23). Humble people are loving, patient, and kind. They are faithful to God, and they have great self-control. We should all strive to have and demonstrate the nine fruits of the Holy Spirit.

Love should be our greatest aim, but humility should be the way we display it. As followers of Christ, we should always strive to walk in the spirit of humility.

I walk in the spirit of humility.

Day 21: Complete In Christ

"For in him we live and move and have our being."
–Acts 17:28

The saddest thing in the world to me is a Christian that places their self-worth in people, places, and things. Why do we allow the world to define who we are when the world didn't create us? We seek validation from things that are mortal when God, who is immortal, created us. The things in this world are temporary and will fade away, but God is eternal and will live on forever.

If you measure your self-value by the world's standards, you will constantly battle feelings of unworthiness, incompletion, and emptiness. The world will make you believe that your value is based on your physical appearance, race, and economic class. The Word tells us in 1 Samuel 16:7, "People judge by outward appearance, but the Lord looks at the heart." God judges our hearts because He knows who we truly are behind the facades we put out to the world.

God made us in His image. And now that we are born again through Jesus Christ, we are united with Him through the Holy Spirit. Colossians 2:10 says, "So you also are complete through your union with Christ, who is the head over every ruler and authority." Your worth, your value, and your self-esteem should be rooted in Christ.

Never forget who you are. You are fearfully and wonderfully made (Psalms 139:14). You are special. You are important. You are wanted. You are needed. You are loved. You are somebody, and your validation comes from God and God only. God loves and adores you. You are complete in Christ.

I am complete in Christ.

Day 22: Fear No More

"For ye have not received the spirit of bondage again to fear; but ye have received the Spirit of adoption, whereby we cry, Abba, Father." –Romans 8:15

You are intelligent, charismatic, and ambitious. So why aren't you further along in life? The answer is simple. You haven't conquered your fears. You have allowed the spirit of fear to paralyze you. So where did this spirit come from because it surely didn't come from God.

2 Timothy 1:7 says "For God hath not given us the spirit of fear; but of power, and of love, and of a sound mind." The enemy plants the spirit of fear in our minds through seeds of doubt, discouragement, and unbelief. Once those seeds become full grown they develop into fear and fear keeps us in bondage.

God wants us to be delivered from the spirit of fear. It is no coincidence that "fear not" is written 366 times in the Bible. For every day of the year, God wants us to live fearlessly. Now that doesn't mean we won't have fears. We all have fears and phobias, but we don't have to let our fears overcome us.

To overcome the spirit fear, you must put your complete trust in God. In Isaiah 41:10 God tells us, "So do not fear, for I am with you; do not be dismayed, for

I am your God. I will strengthen you and help you; I will uphold you with my righteous right hand." When you feel the spirit of fear attacking you, call out to God in prayer. Resist the spirit of fear by praising, worshipping, and speaking God's Word. God has not given you the spirit of fear. He has given you love, power, and a sound mind! You don't have to live in fear anymore.

God has not given me the spirit of fear, but of power, love, and a sound mind.

Day 23: Use Your Gift

"God has given each of you a gift from his great variety
of spiritual gifts. Use them well to serve one another."
–1 Peter 4:10

God has blessed all of us with a special gift, talent, or
ability. In Romans 12:6 it says "We have different gifts,
according to the grace given us." Before we were
formed in our mothers' womb, God knew the plans He
had for us. He predestined our lives and gave each of
us a gift to use for the edifying and building of His
Kingdom.

Our gifts are given to us by the Holy Spirit.
According to Romans 12:3-8 there are seven main
spiritual gifts which include: prophecy, serving,
teaching, encouraging, giving, organizing, and mercy.
In addition to those gifts, we can also receive the gift of
faith, healing, working of miracles, discerning of
spirits, and speaking in tongues (1 Corinthians 12:7-11).

When we mature and develop our gifts, they
can propel us into greatness. The Bible tells us, "A
man's gift makes room for him and brings him before
great men" (Proverbs 18:16). Our gifts, when used to
glorify God, can advance us in our careers, ministries,
and businesses.

Before you were born, God imparted spiritual gifts in your spirit. Your spiritual gifts are eternal and can never be taken away because "the gifts and the calling of God are irrevocable" (Romans 11:29). If you don't know what your spiritual gifts are, ask the Holy Spirit to reveal them to you. Use your gifts because there are people in this world that need them!

I will use my spiritual gifts to serve God and help others.

Day 24: The Real Enemy

"I don't want Satan to outwit us. After all, we are not ignorant about Satan's scheming." -2 Corinthians 2:11

⎧⎰⎞⎝⎱⎫

The Bible tells us to love our enemies (Matthew 5:44). For many people, this is hard to do. I use to struggle with this concept until I got the revelation that people are not my enemies. People are just tools our real enemy uses to fight against us. Who is our enemy? Our real enemy is Satan and his cohorts. Ephesians 6:12 says, "For we are not fighting against flesh-and-blood enemies, but against evil rulers and authorities of the unseen world, against mighty powers in this dark world, and against evil spirits in the heavenly place."

The enemies we fight against are evil spirits. Some people call them demons. Others call them fallen angels. Call them whatever you like, but your mean boss or abusive husband is not your enemy. When people oppose you, it is not the individual that is against you but the spirit inside of them.

Once you grasp that concept, you will learn that you cannot fight a spiritual enemy with physical weapons. Apostle Paul teaches us in 2 Corinthians 10:4, "For the weapons of our warfare are not of the flesh but have divine power to destroy strongholds." God has given us unlimited power and weapons to fight our spiritual enemies. The weapons we use are prayer, praise, worship, fasting, and speaking God's Word.

Remember people are not your enemies. They are just pawns the devil uses to do his bidding. Don't let people make you hate them. Do as the Bible instructs you and pray for your enemies because they need deliverance. Pray they "come to their senses and escape from the devil's trap. For they have been held captive by him to do whatever he wants" (2 Timothy 2:26).

The devil is my real enemy.

Day 25: You Have The Power

"But thanks be to God! He gives us the victory through
our Lord Jesus Christ." –1 Corinthians 15:57

Do you know the power you possess inside of you? The
same power that rose Christ from the dead lives inside
of you. Jesus has given you that power to overcome all
the enemy's lies, schemes, temptations, and attacks. In
Luke 10:19 Jesus says, "Look, I have given you authority
over all the power of the enemy, and you can walk
among snakes and scorpions and crush them. Nothing
will injure you."

Understand, the enemy, is going to attack you.
The enemy tries to engage us in spiritual warfare every
day. That's why the Word tells in 1 Peter 5:8, "Be self-
controlled and alert. Your enemy the devil prowls
around like a roaring lion looking for someone to
devour." Satan hates us and will stop at nothing to
steal from us, kill us, and destroy us (John 10:10).
Though none of us are exempt from his attacks, we can
confidently declare that no weapon he forms against us
will prosper (Isaiah 54:17).

Why will it not prosper? It won't prosper
because Jesus has already defeated him. The Word tells
us in Colossians 2:15, "He disarmed the spiritual rulers
and authorities. He shamed them publicly by his
victory over them on the cross." Because Jesus defeated

Satan on the Cross, we have the power to defeat him as well.

Daily stand on this promise, "For everyone who has been born of God overcomes the world. And this is the victory that has overcome the world—our faith" (1 John 5:4). You have the power to overcome the enemy because greater is He who lives inside of you than the devil who runs and controls this world (1 John 4:4). You are an overcomer, and you have the power!

I have the power through Jesus Christ to overcome the enemy.

Day 26: By Faith

"And my righteous ones will live by faith. But I will
take no pleasure in anyone who turns away."
–Hebrews 10:38

What is faith? According to Hebrews 11:1, "Now faith is
the substance of things hoped for, the evidence of
things not seen." We all know the definition of faith
but are we living by it? We are supposed to live by faith
and not by sight (2 Corinthians 5:7). But most of the
time we live led by our emotions and what see in the
natural realm.

Living by faith requires that we see beyond our
natural eyes. Many times God will show us something
in the spiritual realm before we see it manifest in the
natural. Having real and true faith requires we see a
summer's day on a winter's night. Real faith requires
we see the promise land while we are still in the
wilderness. Real faith decrees and declares that the
bills are already paid even when we don't have the
money. Even when what He showed us seems
impossible to manifest, the faith inside us should rise
up and say, "with man this is impossible, but with God
all things are possible" (Matthew 19:26).

Living by faith is not an option. It is a
requirement mandated by God. In Hebrews 11:6,
Apostle Paul teaches us, "No one can please God

without faith. Whoever goes to God must believe that God exists and that he rewards those who seek him." To develop faith, we must read, study, and meditate on His Word. When we live and act according to our faith, we allow God to do "exceeding abundantly above all that we ask or think, according to the power that works in us" (Ephesians 3:20).

I walk by faith and not by sight.

Day 27: The Right Road

"See, I have set before you today life and good, death and evil." –Deuteronomy 30:15

God has given us a choice to choose life or death, to obey and serve Him and be blessed, or the choice to forsake Him and be cursed. God does not force Himself on us. He gives us the freewill to make choices. Therefore, we must be wise and make the right choice because our very lives depend on it.

In the New Testament, Jesus uses the metaphor of a narrow and wide road to describe the right and wrong choice. "But the gateway to life is very narrow and the road is difficult, and only a few ever find it" (Matthew 7:14). The narrow road leads to heaven and those that travel on its path choose to obey and submit to Christ. The other road, the wide road which leads to hell, is the most commonly traveled road. Those that travel on its path are choosing a life of disobedience and sin. On which road are you traveling?

If you've been disobedient to God's Word and living in sin, I can guarantee you that you are not traveling on the narrow road. God is not going force you to travel on the right road. He will ask you, but He won't beg you. In John 14:15 Jesus said, "If you love me, keep my commands." If you love God, you will choose to be obedient.

I choose to obey God.

Day 28: Rest

"Come to me, all of you who are weary and carry heavy burdens, and I will give you rest." –Matthew 11:28

How many of us think we are superwoman or superman! We think we can do it all, but news flash, we can't. A car that is empty on fuel, no matter how hard you press on the gas, will not go anywhere. Stop trying to drive on low fuel. When you start running low on energy and strength, park your body and take a break.

During Jesus' public ministry He would often slip away from the crowds and rest. In Mark 6:31 Jesus told His disciples, "Let's go off by ourselves to a quiet place and rest awhile." Jesus understood without proper self-care and rest He couldn't effectively minister to anyone and neither can you. I know many people depend on you to be their superman or superwoman, but how can you save them if you can barely fly? You need to rest!

God created one day out of the week for us to rest. This day is the Sabbath Day. Exodus 20:8-10 says, "Remember the Sabbath day, to keep it holy. Six days you shall labor, and do all your work, but the seventh day is a Sabbath to the Lord your God." Most American Christians honor the Sabbath Day on Sunday. Others honor it on Saturday. No matter what day you honor it on, just take that day and rest!

I will rest on the Sabbath Day.

Day 29: Harvest Field

"Ask the Lord of the harvest, therefore, to send out workers into His harvest." –Matthew 9:38

There is a great big harvest field out there filled with lost souls desperately needing to hear about Christ. There are so many people in this world who are lost, broken, and confused. If only someone would witness to them about Christ. Will you be that someone? Before Jesus ascended to heaven, He gave us this command, "Go into all the world and preach the Good News to everyone" (Mark 16:15).

As Christians, we should be trying to win as many souls as we can for the Kingdom of God. In Romans 10:14 Apostle Paul asked, "But how can they call on him to save them unless they believe in him? And how can they believe in him if they have never heard of him? And how can they hear about him unless someone tells them?" Someone at your job, school, or gym needs for you to tell them about Jesus.

Before you were saved someone witnessed to you about Christ; they told you all about His love, freedom, healing, deliverance, and peace. You heard that if you believed in him, you would be forgiven of your sins and receive eternal life. Remember how happy you were? Rekindle the fire you once had and go out and be a soul winner for Christ. Be a worker in God's harvest fields!

I will win souls for Christ.

Day 30: Speak Up For Others

"Defend weak people and orphans. Protect the rights of the oppressed and the poor." –Psalms 82:3

Do you feel a deep compassion towards people less fortunate than you? Do you get angry when you see people being mistreated, abused, hurt, neglected, or abandoned? Do you feel a small tugging at your heart to do or say something about it? The tugging at your heart is God. He is calling you to speak up on behalf of those who cannot speak up for themselves. Proverbs 31:8, "Speak up for those who cannot speak for themselves; ensure justice for those being crushed."

God anointed Moses to save and deliver the Israelites from the Egyptians. He saw how bad they were being treated as slaves and felt compelled to protect and save them. Maybe God has anointed you to do the same. The Word tells us in Isaiah 1:17, "Learn to do right; seek justice. Defend the oppressed. Take up the cause of the fatherless; plead the case of the widow."

There are many ways you can speak up for others. You can start a nonprofit organization, a website, use various social media platforms, or make an informative video. The point is to bring public attention and awareness to a particular person or group of people who cannot speak up for themselves.

God has anointed some of us to speak up for others. He has called us to help those in need. The second greatest commandment is to love your neighbor as you love yourself (Matthew 22:39). Some of our brothers and sisters in Christ need our guidance and direction. They need our voice. If you feel the tugging at your heart, answer the call.

I will speak up for others in need.

Day 31: The Ultimate Sacrifice

"I have been crucified with Christ, and I no longer live, but Christ lives in me. The life I now live in the body, I live by faith in the Son of God, who loved me and gave himself for me." –Galatians 2:20

Our Lord and Savior Jesus Christ hung, bled, and died upon the Cross for our sins. His sacrifice carried our grief, sorrows, and afflictions. He was wounded for our transgressions, and by His stripes, we are healed (Isaiah 53:5). Christ endured the Cross so that we may have eternal life. We can never repay Him back for His ultimate sacrifice on Calvary, but we can make a choice to follow in His footsteps and dedicate our lives to Him.

In Luke 9:23, Jesus says, "If any of you want to be my follower, you must turn from your selfish ways, take up your cross daily, and follow me." To follow Christ means we have to crucify our flesh daily. In some cases, it means we have to give up everything we own. Nobody knows this better than a young rich man in the Bible. In Mark 10 it recounts a story about a young man and his quest to inherit eternal life.

One day while Jesus was setting out on a journey a young rich man approached Him and asked Him how he could receive enteral life. Jesus told the man if he wanted to inherit eternal life he had to go and sell all his possessions and give the money to the poor and then follow Him (Mark 10:21). Did he make the ultimate sacrifice and do as Jesus instructed Him? Mark 10:22 says, "At this, the man's face fell, and he went away sad, for he had many possessions." Unfortunately, he did not.

If Jesus asked you to make the ultimate sacrifice would you do it? Jesus assures, "no one who has left house or brothers or sisters or mother or father or children or lands, for my sake and for the gospel, who will not receive a hundredfold now in this time, houses and brothers and sisters and mothers and children and lands, with persecutions, and in the age to come eternal life." Mark 10:29-30.

Make the ultimate sacrifice and give up your life for the sake of Christ. His plans for you are far greater and better than you could ever imagine.

I will give up my life and follow Christ.

Your Journey Continues

"Seek the Lord and his strength; seek his presence
continually!" –1 Chronicles 6:11

You did it! You completed your 31 days, but your
journey continues. Seeking God shouldn't be done
casually or end with this book. My prayer is that the
devotionals in this book kindled a deeper desire in
your spirit to seek God more fervently. To help you
continue on your journey, I have written this daily
model prayer. Pray this prayer every morning when
you wake up and remember to seek Him early, seek
Him first, and seek Him always!

Dear Heavenly Father,

Thank you for waking me up this morning and
allowing me to see another day.

As I rise, I give you the praise, honor, and glory due
unto your name.

For you are worthy to be praised and I will bless your
name at all times.

I know that it is your grace, mercy, compassion, and
loving kindness that sustains me.

Forgive me of my sins as I forgive others who have
sinned against me.

Before I start my day, I ask that you give me my daily bread and order my steps in your Word.

Help me walk my faith and not by sight.

Supply all my needs according to your riches in glory in your son Christ Jesus.

Impart into me a spirit of wisdom and revelation to complete my daily tasks.

Give me clarity when I get confused and strengthen me when I get weak.

Send your angels to encamp all around me and protect me from danger seen and unseen.

Bless my family, friends, as well as my enemies.

Give me words of encouragement to all who cross my path and use me to spread the Good News to those that are lost.

Let no weapon formed against me prosper and condemn every tongue that rises against me in judgment.

I seal this prayer by the Blood of Lamb and the word of my testimony.

In Jesus name, I pray, Amen.

10 Scriptures to Remember

"But seek ye first the kingdom of God, and his righteousness; and all these things shall be added unto you."

–Matthew 6:33

"For God so loved the world, that he gave his only begotten Son, that whosoever believeth in him should not perish, but have everlasting life."

–John 3:16

"I will bless the LORD at all times; his praise shall continually be in my mouth."

–Psalms 34:1

"I can do all things through Christ which strengthens me."

–Philippians 4:13

"For we wrestle not against flesh and blood, but against principalities, against powers, against the rulers of the darkness of this world, against spiritual wickedness in high places."

–Ephesians 6:12

"Behold, I give unto you power to tread on serpents and scorpions, and over all the power of the enemy: and nothing shall by any means hurt you."

–Luke 10:19

"Be careful for nothing, but in everything by prayer and supplication with thanksgiving let your requests be made known unto God. And the peace of God, which passeth all understanding, shall keep your hearts and minds through Christ Jesus."

–Philippians 4:6-7

"But my God shall supply all your need according to his riches in glory by Christ Jesus."

–Philippians 4:19

"But he was wounded for our transgressions; he was bruised for our iniquities: the chastisement of our peace was upon him, and with his stripes, we are healed."

–Isaiah 53:5

"Praying always with all prayer and supplication in the Spirit, and watching thereunto with all perseverance and supplication for all saints."

–Ephesians 6:18

Order Form

www.ingramcontent.com/pod-product-compliance
Lightning Source LLC
Chambersburg PA
CBHW062025040426
42447CB00010B/2140